Big Dreams, Daily Joys Journal

Elise Blaha Cripe

CHRONICLE BOOKS

SAN FRANCISCO

Ready to dream bigger and find daily joy?

THIS JOURNAL IS DESIGNED TO HELP you make progress on your goals, assess how things are going on a weekly basis, and build a life that you enjoy.

This method is just one way to stay on track and get things done, and this journal, like a hammer or a keyboard, is just a tool. It's not a magic wand or a lottery ticket. *You* are going to do the reflection. *You* are going to set the goals. *You* are going to make the progress.

Over the next few weeks, months, and years, this journal will be a guide and a witness to your growth and change. Please use it!

How to get the most from this journal

The point of planning isn't to schedule every moment of our days. In fact, the point of planning is to make sure we don't end up doing something every moment of every day.

Typically, when we think about planning, we look forward: What do I need to do tomorrow? Next week? This month? While this is important, it's equally important to look backward.

This journal helps you do that.

What you'll find in these pages

Each week, you are invited to check in and evaluate what you are currently doing and what you need to be doing to reach your big and small goals. You can pick any day to do this. Maybe you find it helpful to reflect on Friday afternoons before heading into the weekend. Or maybe it's better for you to carve out a few minutes Sunday evening. When you make the time doesn't matter, but try to find a time in your schedule that you can repeat on a weekly basis.

Why reflect? Why goal-set?

It can be really easy to get caught up in day-to-day hustle, where it feels like you are always moving but never really getting anywhere. This journal asks you to hop out of the race for just a few minutes each week and check in. Where have you been these past seven days? Where are you hoping to go in the next seven?

Think of your weekly check-ins as an opportunity to both reflect and goal-set. This is a chance to remind yourself that you're on a path. That path isn't a straight line. Sometimes it's a slog. Sometimes it's a sprint. But it's *your* path. You get to make it work for you. Let this journal help you build your own personal map.

Like any exercise, this only works if you do it. And you're only going to want to take this time if you can create a nonjudgmental space for yourself each check-in. Be honest with how last week went! Be realistic about what you can accomplish next week! And give yourself grace as you evaluate where you are at. This journal is for you alone. No one will see what you did (or didn't do). You can't "win" or "lose," but you can keep showing up.

Reflect

Look back and think carefully about the past week.

First, each entry will ask you to take a few minutes to look backward. This section is divided into three areas that will help you see what you've accomplished, what you're still making progress on, and what you need to let go of.

What were your wins last week?

What you write down here will vary. Some weeks it might be small things. (You turned in the library books on time! You stayed on top of the laundry!) Other weeks you may have bigger milestones. (You got a raise at work! You threw a party for your best friend!) Everything counts! Big or small, write it down.

Often our days pass in such a blur that we forget to celebrate these important wins because it feels like there is so much still left on our plate. Sometimes it feels like our lists will never run out and we will be spinning our wheels for the rest of time.

Taking a few minutes each week to sit down and think back on what we actually got done is a way to stop those spinning wheels for a moment. This exercise, no matter what you wrote, should feel encouraging and rewarding. Taking these minutes won't make your to-do list shorter, but it will make your attitude toward it better.

What are you still working on?

Next, you'll be asked to document what is still in progress. What projects did you get started on that you haven't yet finished? What are you carrying over from last week (or the week prior)? Get those items on paper.

What do you need to let go of?

And finally, as you reflect back on the past week, is there anything you need to forget about?

Sometimes this might be a literal thing, like that sweater you shrunk in the wash. Other times it might be an idea or project that you've realized isn't going to work out. Or it might be a comment you got from your coworker that irked you and is sitting in the back of your mind and you can't forget about.

Hanging on to stuff that isn't working is like letting a black cloud hang over your head, which can be a hindrance to your overall productivity. This part of the reflection is important to create more space. Letting go of both literal and figurative things makes room for the ideas and work you are really passionate about.

Goal-Set

Look forward and come up with your realistic intentions for the next week.

Next, after your reflection period, the journal will ask you to take a few minutes to look forward. This section is divided into three areas that will help you to prioritize your list so you know where to focus your energy and time.

What do you need to complete in the week ahead?

First, what has to get done, both personally and professionally? This section is for the most important stuff that is actually due this coming week. These could be complicated and involved projects, like preparing to move, or small but necessary items, like scheduling a dentist appointment. The items on this list are what you want to accomplish first.

What do you need to work on?

Next are the items you would love to make progress on but that are not due or urgent to finish in the next week. An example might be cleaning out your pantry, pulling weeds from the backyard, or updating all the copy on your website. Again, these items are not yet your main focus, but they might be the projects on your "must complete list" a few weeks from now.

What are you thinking about?

And finally, what's on your mind as you enter this week? These are the items that are not due yet, not even in progress, but just ideas that could use some percolating. This could be anything from a product idea you had in the shower this morning to a paint color you're thinking about for your bedroom. Get those thoughts and ideas out of your mind and onto paper.

Date:

Reflect

What were your wins last week? _____

_____

_____

_____

_____

_____

What are you still working on? _____

_____

_____

_____

_____

What do you need to let go of? _____

_____

_____

_____

_____

Goal-Set

What do you need to complete in the week ahead? _____

_____

_____

_____

_____

_____

What do you need to work on? _____

_____

_____

_____

_____

_____

What are you thinking about? _____

_____

_____

_____

_____

_____

Start today

Date:

Reflect

What were your wins last week? _____

_____

_____

_____

_____

_____

What are you still working on? _____

_____

_____

_____

_____

_____

What do you need to let go of? _____

_____

_____

_____

_____

_____

Goal-Set

What do you need to complete in the week ahead? _____

_____

_____

_____

_____

_____

What do you need to work on? _____

_____

_____

_____

_____

What are you thinking about? _____

_____

_____

_____

_____

Date:

Reflect

What were your wins last week? _____

_____

_____

_____

_____

_____

What are you still working on? _____

_____

_____

_____

_____

_____

What do you need to let go of? _____

_____

_____

_____

_____

_____

Goal-Set

What do you need to complete in the week ahead? _____

_____

_____

_____

_____

_____

What do you need to work on? _____

_____

_____

_____

_____

What are you thinking about? _____

_____

_____

_____

_____

Date:

Reflect

What were your wins last week? _____

_____

_____

_____

_____

_____

What are you still working on? _____

_____

_____

_____

_____

_____

What do you need to let go of? _____

_____

_____

_____

_____

_____

Goal-Set

What do you need to complete in the week ahead? _____

_____

_____

_____

_____

_____

What do you need to work on? _____

_____

_____

_____

_____

What are you thinking about? _____

_____

_____

_____

_____

Progress > perfection

Date:

Reflect

What were your wins last week? _____

_____

_____

_____

_____

_____

What are you still working on? _____

_____

_____

_____

_____

_____

What do you need to let go of? _____

_____

_____

_____

_____

_____

Goal-Set

What do you need to complete in the week ahead? _____

_____

_____

_____

_____

_____

What do you need to work on? _____

_____

_____

_____

_____

What are you thinking about? _____

_____

_____

_____

_____

Reflect

What were your wins last week? _____

_____

_____

_____

_____

_____

What are you still working on? _____

_____

_____

_____

_____

What do you need to let go of? _____

_____

_____

_____

_____

Goal-Set

What do you need to complete in the week ahead? _____

_____

_____

_____

_____

_____

What do you need to work on? _____

_____

_____

_____

_____

What are you thinking about? _____

_____

_____

_____

_____

_____

Date:

Reflect

What were your wins last week? _____

_____

_____

_____

_____

_____

What are you still working on? _____

_____

_____

_____

_____

What do you need to let go of? _____

_____

_____

_____

_____

Goal-Set

What do you need to complete in the week ahead? _____

_____

_____

_____

_____

_____

What do you need to work on? _____

_____

_____

_____

_____

_____

What are you thinking about? _____

_____

_____

_____

_____

_____

Get it done

Date:

Reflect

What were your wins last week? _____

_____
_____
_____
_____
_____

What are you still working on? _____

_____
_____
_____
_____

What do you need to let go of? _____

_____
_____
_____
_____

Goal-Set

What do you need to complete in the week ahead? _____

_____

_____

_____

_____

What do you need to work on? _____

_____

_____

_____

_____

What are you thinking about? _____

_____

_____

_____

_____

Reflect

What were your wins last week? _____

_____

_____

_____

_____

_____

What are you still working on? _____

_____

_____

_____

_____

_____

What do you need to let go of? _____

_____

_____

_____

_____

_____

Goal-Set

What do you need to complete in the week ahead? _____

_____

_____

_____

_____

_____

What do you need to work on? _____

_____

_____

_____

_____

_____

What are you thinking about? _____

_____

_____

_____

_____

_____

Reflect

What were your wins last week? _____

_____

_____

_____

_____

_____

What are you still working on? _____

_____

_____

_____

_____

_____

What do you need to let go of? _____

_____

_____

_____

_____

_____

Goal-Set

What do you need to complete in the week ahead? _____

_____

_____

_____

_____

_____

What do you need to work on? _____

_____

_____

_____

_____

_____

What are you thinking about? _____

_____

_____

_____

_____

_____

Date:

Reflect

What were your wins last week? _____

_____

_____

_____

_____

_____

What are you still working on? _____

_____

_____

_____

_____

What do you need to let go of? _____

_____

_____

_____

_____

_____

Goal-Set

What do you need to complete in the week ahead? _____

_____

_____

_____

_____

_____

What do you need to work on? _____

_____

_____

_____

_____

What are you thinking about? _____

_____

_____

_____

_____

Everything is possible

Date:

Reflect

What were your wins last week? _____

_____

_____

_____

_____

_____

What are you still working on? _____

_____

_____

_____

_____

_____

What do you need to let go of? _____

_____

_____

_____

_____

_____

Goal-Set

What do you need to complete in the week ahead? _____

_____

_____

_____

_____

_____

What do you need to work on? _____

_____

_____

_____

_____

_____

What are you thinking about? _____

_____

_____

_____

_____

_____

Reflect

What were your wins last week? _____

_____

_____

_____

_____

_____

What are you still working on? _____

_____

_____

_____

_____

_____

What do you need to let go of? _____

_____

_____

_____

_____

_____

Goal-Set

What do you need to complete in the week ahead? _____

_____

_____

_____

_____

_____

What do you need to work on? _____

_____

_____

_____

_____

_____

What are you thinking about? _____

_____

_____

_____

_____

_____

Date:

Reflect

What were your wins last week? _____

_____

_____

_____

_____

_____

What are you still working on? _____

_____

_____

_____

_____

_____

What do you need to let go of? _____

_____

_____

_____

_____

_____

Goal-Set

What do you need to complete in the week ahead? _____

_____

_____

_____

_____

_____

What do you need to work on? _____

_____

_____

_____

_____

_____

What are you thinking about? _____

_____

_____

_____

_____

_____

You're doing a great job

Reflect

What were your wins last week? _____

_____

_____

_____

_____

_____

What are you still working on? _____

_____

_____

_____

_____

_____

What do you need to let go of? _____

_____

_____

_____

_____

Goal-Set

What do you need to complete in the week ahead? _____

_____

_____

_____

_____

_____

What do you need to work on? _____

_____

_____

_____

_____

_____

What are you thinking about? _____

_____

_____

_____

_____

_____

Date:

Reflect

What were your wins last week? _____

_____

_____

_____

_____

_____

What are you still working on? _____

_____

_____

_____

_____

_____

What do you need to let go of? _____

_____

_____

_____

_____

_____

Goal-Set

What do you need to complete in the week ahead? _____

_____

_____

_____

_____

_____

What do you need to work on? _____

_____

_____

_____

_____

_____

What are you thinking about? _____

_____

_____

_____

_____

_____

Date:

Reflect

What were your wins last week? _____
_____
_____
_____
_____
_____

What are you still working on? _____
_____
_____
_____
_____

What do you need to let go of? _____
_____
_____
_____
_____

Goal-Set

What do you need to complete in the week ahead? _____

_____

_____

_____

_____

_____

What do you need to work on? _____

_____

_____

_____

_____

_____

What are you thinking about? _____

_____

_____

_____

_____

Date:

Reflect

What were your wins last week? _____

_____

_____

_____

_____

_____

What are you still working on? _____

_____

_____

_____

_____

What do you need to let go of? _____

_____

_____

_____

_____

Goal-Set

What do you need to complete in the week ahead? _____

_____

_____

_____

_____

_____

What do you need to work on? _____

_____

_____

_____

_____

What are you thinking about? _____

_____

_____

_____

_____

Take it one day at a time

Reflect

What were your wins last week? _____

_____

_____

_____

_____

_____

What are you still working on? _____

_____

_____

_____

_____

_____

What do you need to let go of? _____

_____

_____

_____

_____

_____

Goal-Set

What do you need to complete in the week ahead? _____

_____

_____

_____

_____

_____

What do you need to work on? _____

_____

_____

_____

_____

_____

What are you thinking about? _____

_____

_____

_____

_____

_____

Date:

Reflect

What were your wins last week? _____

_____

_____

_____

_____

_____

What are you still working on? _____

_____

_____

_____

_____

_____

What do you need to let go of? _____

_____

_____

_____

_____

_____

Goal-Set

What do you need to complete in the week ahead? _____

_____

_____

_____

_____

_____

What do you need to work on? _____

_____

_____

_____

_____

_____

What are you thinking about? _____

_____

_____

_____

_____

_____

Date:

Reflect

What were your wins last week? _____

_____

_____

_____

_____

_____

What are you still working on? _____

_____

_____

_____

_____

What do you need to let go of? _____

_____

_____

_____

_____

Goal-Set

What do you need to complete in the week ahead? _____

_____

_____

_____

_____

_____

What do you need to work on? _____

_____

_____

_____

_____

_____

What are you thinking about? _____

_____

_____

_____

_____

Make today better than yesterday

Date:

Reflect

What were your wins last week? _____
_____
_____
_____
_____
_____

What are you still working on? _____
_____
_____
_____
_____

What do you need to let go of? _____
_____
_____
_____
_____
_____

Goal-Set

What do you need to complete in the week ahead? _____

_____

_____

_____

_____

_____

What do you need to work on? _____

_____

_____

_____

_____

_____

What are you thinking about? _____

_____

_____

_____

_____

_____

Date:

Reflect

What were your wins last week? _____
_____
_____
_____
_____
_____
_____

What are you still working on? _____
_____
_____
_____
_____
_____

What do you need to let go of? _____
_____
_____
_____
_____
_____

Goal-Set

What do you need to complete in the week ahead? _____

_____

_____

_____

_____

_____

What do you need to work on? _____

_____

_____

_____

_____

What are you thinking about? _____

_____

_____

_____

_____

Date:

Reflect

What were your wins last week? _____

_____

_____

_____

_____

_____

What are you still working on? _____

_____

_____

_____

_____

What do you need to let go of? _____

_____

_____

_____

_____

Goal-Set

What do you need to complete in the week ahead? _____

_____

_____

_____

_____

_____

What do you need to work on? _____

_____

_____

_____

_____

_____

What are you thinking about? _____

_____

_____

_____

_____

_____

You're not going to run out of ideas

Date:

Reflect

What were your wins last week? _____

_____

_____

_____

_____

_____

What are you still working on? _____

_____

_____

_____

_____

What do you need to let go of? _____

_____

_____

_____

_____

Goal-Set

What do you need to complete in the week ahead? _____

_____

_____

_____

_____

_____

What do you need to work on? _____

_____

_____

_____

_____

What are you thinking about? _____

_____

_____

_____

_____

Reflect

What were your wins last week? _____

_____

_____

_____

_____

_____

What are you still working on? _____

_____

_____

_____

_____

_____

What do you need to let go of? _____

_____

_____

_____

_____

_____

Goal-Set

What do you need to complete in the week ahead? _____

_____

_____

_____

_____

_____

What do you need to work on? _____

_____

_____

_____

_____

What are you thinking about? _____

_____

_____

_____

_____

Date:

Reflect

What were your wins last week? _____

_____

_____

_____

_____

_____

What are you still working on? _____

_____

_____

_____

_____

What do you need to let go of? _____

_____

_____

_____

_____

Goal-Set

What do you need to complete in the week ahead? _____

_____

_____

_____

_____

_____

What do you need to work on? _____

_____

_____

_____

_____

What are you thinking about? _____

_____

_____

_____

_____

Think big!

Date:

Reflect

What were your wins last week? _____

_____
_____
_____
_____
_____

What are you still working on? _____

_____
_____
_____
_____
_____

What do you need to let go of? _____

_____
_____
_____
_____
_____

Goal-Set

What do you need to complete in the week ahead? _____

_____

_____

_____

_____

_____

What do you need to work on? _____

_____

_____

_____

_____

_____

What are you thinking about? _____

_____

_____

_____

_____

Date:

Reflect

What were your wins last week? _____

_____

_____

_____

_____

_____

What are you still working on? _____

_____

_____

_____

_____

_____

What do you need to let go of? _____

_____

_____

_____

_____

_____

Goal-Set

What do you need to complete in the week ahead? _____

_____

_____

_____

_____

_____

What do you need to work on? _____

_____

_____

_____

_____

_____

What are you thinking about? _____

_____

_____

_____

_____

_____

Reflect

What were your wins last week? _____

_____

_____

_____

_____

_____

What are you still working on? _____

_____

_____

_____

_____

_____

What do you need to let go of? _____

_____

_____

_____

_____

_____

Goal-Set

What do you need to complete in the week ahead? _____

_____

_____

_____

_____

What do you need to work on? _____

_____

_____

_____

_____

What are you thinking about? _____

_____

_____

_____

_____

You have enough time

Reflect

What were your wins last week? _____

_____

_____

_____

_____

_____

What are you still working on? _____

_____

_____

_____

_____

_____

What do you need to let go of? _____

_____

_____

_____

_____

_____

Goal-Set

What do you need to complete in the week ahead? _____

_____

_____

_____

_____

_____

What do you need to work on? _____

_____

_____

_____

_____

_____

What are you thinking about? _____

_____

_____

_____

_____

Reflect

What were your wins last week? _____

_____

_____

_____

_____

_____

What are you still working on? _____

_____

_____

_____

_____

_____

What do you need to let go of? _____

_____

_____

_____

_____

_____

Goal-Set

What do you need to complete in the week ahead? _____

_____

_____

_____

_____

_____

What do you need to work on? _____

_____

_____

_____

_____

_____

What are you thinking about? _____

_____

_____

_____

_____

_____

Reflect

What were your wins last week? _____

_____

_____

_____

_____

_____

What are you still working on? _____

_____

_____

_____

_____

What do you need to let go of? _____

_____

_____

_____

_____

Goal-Set

What do you need to complete in the week ahead? _____

_____

_____

_____

_____

_____

What do you need to work on? _____

_____

_____

_____

_____

_____

What are you thinking about? _____

_____

_____

_____

_____

_____

Date:

Reflect

What were your wins last week? _____

_____

_____

_____

_____

_____

What are you still working on? _____

_____

_____

_____

_____

What do you need to let go of? _____

_____

_____

_____

_____

Goal-Set

What do you need to complete in the week ahead? _____

_____

_____

_____

_____

_____

What do you need to work on? _____

_____

_____

_____

_____

_____

What are you thinking about? _____

_____

_____

_____

_____

_____

If you don't like it, change it

Date:

Reflect

What were your wins last week? _____

_____
_____
_____
_____
_____

What are you still working on? _____

_____
_____
_____
_____
_____

What do you need to let go of? _____

_____
_____
_____
_____
_____

Goal-Set

What do you need to complete in the week ahead? _____

_____

_____

_____

_____

_____

What do you need to work on? _____

_____

_____

_____

_____

What are you thinking about? _____

_____

_____

_____

_____

Reflect

What were your wins last week? _____

_____

_____

_____

_____

_____

What are you still working on? _____

_____

_____

_____

_____

What do you need to let go of? _____

_____

_____

_____

_____

Goal-Set

What do you need to complete in the week ahead? _____

_____

_____

_____

_____

_____

What do you need to work on? _____

_____

_____

_____

_____

What are you thinking about? _____

_____

_____

_____

_____

Date:

Reflect

What were your wins last week? _____

_____

_____

_____

_____

_____

What are you still working on? _____

_____

_____

_____

_____

_____

What do you need to let go of? _____

_____

_____

_____

_____

_____

Goal-Set

What do you need to complete in the week ahead? _____

_____

_____

_____

_____

_____

What do you need to work on? _____

_____

_____

_____

_____

_____

What are you thinking about? _____

_____

_____

_____

_____

_____

Date:

Reflect

What were your wins last week? _____

_____

_____

_____

_____

_____

What are you still working on? _____

_____

_____

_____

_____

_____

What do you need to let go of? _____

_____

_____

_____

_____

_____

Goal-Set

What do you need to complete in the week ahead? _____

_____

_____

_____

_____

_____

What do you need to work on? _____

_____

_____

_____

_____

What are you thinking about? _____

_____

_____

_____

_____

_____

Start where you are

Date:

Reflect

What were your wins last week? _____
_____
_____
_____
_____
_____

What are you still working on? _____
_____
_____
_____
_____

What do you need to let go of? _____
_____
_____
_____
_____

Goal-Set

What do you need to complete in the week ahead? _____

_____

_____

_____

_____

_____

What do you need to work on? _____

_____

_____

_____

_____

_____

What are you thinking about? _____

_____

_____

_____

_____

_____

Date:

Reflect

What were your wins last week? _____

_____
_____
_____
_____
_____

What are you still working on? _____

_____
_____
_____
_____
_____

What do you need to let go of? _____

_____
_____
_____
_____
_____

Goal-Set

What do you need to complete in the week ahead? _____

_____

_____

_____

_____

_____

What do you need to work on? _____

_____

_____

_____

_____

What are you thinking about? _____

_____

_____

_____

_____

Date:

Reflect

What were your wins last week? _____

_____

_____

_____

_____

_____

What are you still working on? _____

_____

_____

_____

_____

_____

What do you need to let go of? _____

_____

_____

_____

_____

_____

Goal-Set

What do you need to complete in the week ahead? _____

_____

_____

_____

_____

_____

What do you need to work on? _____

_____

_____

_____

_____

_____

What are you thinking about? _____

_____

_____

_____

_____

_____

Reflect

What were your wins last week? _____

_____

_____

_____

_____

_____

What are you still working on? _____

_____

_____

_____

_____

_____

What do you need to let go of? _____

_____

_____

_____

_____

_____

Goal-Set

What do you need to complete in the week ahead? _____

_____

_____

_____

_____

_____

What do you need to work on? _____

_____

_____

_____

_____

What are you thinking about? _____

_____

_____

_____

_____

_____

Do what you can and be done

Date:

Reflect

What were your wins last week? _____

_____

_____

_____

_____

_____

What are you still working on? _____

_____

_____

_____

_____

What do you need to let go of? _____

_____

_____

_____

_____

Goal-Set

What do you need to complete in the week ahead? _____

_____

_____

_____

_____

_____

What do you need to work on? _____

_____

_____

_____

_____

_____

What are you thinking about? _____

_____

_____

_____

_____

_____

Date:

Reflect

What were your wins last week? _____

_____

_____

_____

_____

_____

What are you still working on? _____

_____

_____

_____

_____

_____

What do you need to let go of? _____

_____

_____

_____

_____

Goal-Set

What do you need to complete in the week ahead? _____

_____

_____

_____

_____

_____

What do you need to work on? _____

_____

_____

_____

_____

What are you thinking about? _____

_____

_____

_____

_____

Date:

Reflect

What were your wins last week?

_____

_____

_____

_____

_____

_____

What are you still working on?

_____

_____

_____

_____

_____

What do you need to let go of?

_____

_____

_____

_____

_____

Goal-Set

What do you need to complete in the week ahead? _____

_____

_____

_____

_____

_____

What do you need to work on? _____

_____

_____

_____

_____

What are you thinking about? _____

_____

_____

_____

_____

Don't wait for permission

Date:

Reflect

What were your wins last week? _____

_____

_____

_____

_____

_____

What are you still working on? _____

_____

_____

_____

_____

_____

What do you need to let go of? _____

_____

_____

_____

_____

_____

Goal-Set

What do you need to complete in the week ahead? _____

_____

_____

_____

_____

_____

_____

What do you need to work on? _____

_____

_____

_____

_____

_____

What are you thinking about? _____

_____

_____

_____

_____

_____

Date:

Reflect

What were your wins last week? _____

_____

_____

_____

_____

_____

What are you still working on? _____

_____

_____

_____

_____

What do you need to let go of? _____

_____

_____

_____

_____

Goal-Set

What do you need to complete in the week ahead? _____

_____

_____

_____

_____

_____

What do you need to work on? _____

_____

_____

_____

_____

_____

What are you thinking about? _____

_____

_____

_____

_____

_____

Date:

Reflect

What were your wins last week? _____

_____

_____

_____

_____

_____

What are you still working on? _____

_____

_____

_____

_____

What do you need to let go of? _____

_____

_____

_____

_____

_____

Goal-Set

What do you need to complete in the week ahead? _____

_____

_____

_____

_____

_____

What do you need to work on? _____

_____

_____

_____

_____

_____

What are you thinking about? _____

_____

_____

_____

_____

_____

Trust your process

Date:

Reflect

What were your wins last week? _____

_____

_____

_____

_____

_____

What are you still working on? _____

_____

_____

_____

_____

What do you need to let go of? _____

_____

_____

_____

_____

Goal-Set

What do you need to complete in the week ahead? _____

_____

_____

_____

_____

_____

What do you need to work on? _____

_____

_____

_____

_____

_____

What are you thinking about? _____

_____

_____

_____

_____

_____

Reflect

What were your wins last week? _____
_____
_____
_____
_____
_____

What are you still working on? _____
_____
_____
_____
_____

What do you need to let go of? _____
_____
_____
_____
_____

Goal-Set

What do you need to complete in the week ahead? _____

_____

_____

_____

_____

_____

What do you need to work on? _____

_____

_____

_____

_____

_____

What are you thinking about? _____

_____

_____

_____

_____

_____

Date:

Reflect

What were your wins last week? _____

_____

_____

_____

_____

_____

What are you still working on? _____

_____

_____

_____

_____

_____

What do you need to let go of? _____

_____

_____

_____

_____

_____

Goal-Set

What do you need to complete in the week ahead? _____

_____

_____

_____

_____

_____

What do you need to work on? _____

_____

_____

_____

_____

What are you thinking about? _____

_____

_____

_____

_____

Do your best

Date:

Reflect

What were your wins last week? _____

_____

_____

_____

_____

_____

What are you still working on? _____

_____

_____

_____

_____

What do you need to let go of? _____

_____

_____

_____

_____

Goal-Set

What do you need to complete in the week ahead? _____

_____

_____

_____

_____

What do you need to work on? _____

_____

_____

_____

_____

What are you thinking about? _____

_____

_____

_____

_____

Date:

Reflect

What were your wins last week? _____

_____

_____

_____

_____

_____

What are you still working on? _____

_____

_____

_____

_____

_____

What do you need to let go of? _____

_____

_____

_____

_____

_____

Goal-Set

What do you need to complete in the week ahead? _____

_____

_____

_____

_____

_____

What do you need to work on? _____

_____

_____

_____

_____

_____

What are you thinking about? _____

_____

_____

_____

_____

_____

Date:

Reflect

What were your wins last week?

_____

_____
_____
_____
_____
_____

What are you still working on?

_____

_____
_____
_____
_____
_____

What do you need to let go of?

_____

_____
_____
_____
_____
_____

Goal-Set

What do you need to complete in the week ahead? _____

_____
_____
_____
_____
_____

What do you need to work on? _____

_____
_____
_____
_____
_____

What are you thinking about? _____

_____
_____
_____
_____
_____

Find your step one

Reflect

What were your wins last week? _____

_____

_____

_____

_____

_____

What are you still working on? _____

_____

_____

_____

_____

What do you need to let go of? _____

_____

_____

_____

_____

Goal-Set

What do you need to complete in the week ahead? _____

_____

_____

_____

_____

_____

What do you need to work on? _____

_____

_____

_____

_____

What are you thinking about? _____

_____

_____

_____

_____

Reflect

What were your wins last week? _____

_____
_____
_____
_____
_____

What are you still working on? _____

_____
_____
_____
_____
_____

What do you need to let go of? _____

_____
_____
_____
_____
_____

Goal-Set

What do you need to complete in the week ahead? _____

_____

_____

_____

_____

_____

What do you need to work on? _____

_____

_____

_____

_____

What are you thinking about? _____

_____

_____

_____

_____

Date:

Reflect

What were your wins last week? _____

_____

_____

_____

_____

_____

What are you still working on? _____

_____

_____

_____

_____

_____

What do you need to let go of? _____

_____

_____

_____

_____

_____

Goal-Set

What do you need to complete in the week ahead? _____

_____

_____

_____

_____

_____

What do you need to work on? _____

_____

_____

_____

_____

_____

What are you thinking about? _____

_____

_____

_____

_____

_____

Reflect

What were your wins last week? _____

_____

_____

_____

_____

_____

What are you still working on? _____

_____

_____

_____

_____

What do you need to let go of? _____

_____

_____

_____

_____

Goal-Set

What do you need to complete in the week ahead? _____

_____

_____

_____

_____

_____

What do you need to work on? _____

_____

_____

_____

_____

_____

What are you thinking about? _____

_____

_____

_____

_____

_____

Show up and work hard

Date:

Reflect

What were your wins last week? _____

_____

_____

_____

_____

_____

What are you still working on? _____

_____

_____

_____

_____

What do you need to let go of? _____

_____

_____

_____

_____

Goal-Set

What do you need to complete in the week ahead? _____

_____

_____

_____

_____

_____

What do you need to work on? _____

_____

_____

_____

_____

_____

What are you thinking about? _____

_____

_____

_____

_____

_____

Date:

Reflect

What were your wins last week? _____

_____

_____

_____

_____

_____

What are you still working on? _____

_____

_____

_____

_____

What do you need to let go of? _____

_____

_____

_____

_____

Goal-Set

What do you need to complete in the week ahead? _____

_____

_____

_____

_____

_____

What do you need to work on? _____

_____

_____

_____

_____

_____

What are you thinking about? _____

_____

_____

_____

_____

_____

Date:

Reflect

What were your wins last week? _____

_____
_____
_____
_____
_____

What are you still working on? _____

_____
_____
_____
_____

What do you need to let go of? _____

_____
_____
_____
_____

Goal-Set

What do you need to complete in the week ahead? _____

_____

_____

_____

_____

_____

What do you need to work on? _____

_____

_____

_____

_____

_____

What are you thinking about? _____

_____

_____

_____

_____

_____

Only action drives change

Date:

Reflect

What were your wins last week? _____

_____

_____

_____

_____

_____

What are you still working on? _____

_____

_____

_____

_____

What do you need to let go of? _____

_____

_____

_____

_____

Goal-Set

What do you need to complete in the week ahead? _____

_____

_____

_____

_____

_____

What do you need to work on? _____

_____

_____

_____

_____

What are you thinking about? _____

_____

_____

_____

_____

Date:

Reflect

What were your wins last week? _____

_____

_____

_____

_____

_____

What are you still working on? _____

_____

_____

_____

_____

_____

What do you need to let go of? _____

_____

_____

_____

_____

Goal-Set

What do you need to complete in the week ahead? _____

_____

_____

_____

_____

_____

_____

What do you need to work on? _____

_____

_____

_____

_____

_____

What are you thinking about? _____

_____

_____

_____

_____

_____

Date:

Reflect

What were your wins last week? _____

_____

_____

_____

_____

_____

What are you still working on? _____

_____

_____

_____

_____

_____

What do you need to let go of? _____

_____

_____

_____

_____

_____

Goal-Set

What do you need to complete in the week ahead? _____

_____

_____

_____

_____

_____

What do you need to work on? _____

_____

_____

_____

_____

What are you thinking about? _____

_____

_____

_____

_____

Date:

Reflect

What were your wins last week? _____

_____

_____

_____

_____

_____

What are you still working on? _____

_____

_____

_____

_____

_____

What do you need to let go of? _____

_____

_____

_____

_____

_____

Goal-Set

What do you need to complete in the week ahead? _____

_____

_____

_____

_____

_____

What do you need to work on? _____

_____

_____

_____

_____

_____

What are you thinking about? _____

_____

_____

_____

_____

_____

Practice makes better

Date:

Reflect

What were your wins last week? _____

_____

_____

_____

_____

_____

What are you still working on? _____

_____

_____

_____

_____

_____

What do you need to let go of? _____

_____

_____

_____

_____

_____

Goal-Set

What do you need to complete in the week ahead? _____

_____

_____

_____

_____

_____

What do you need to work on? _____

_____

_____

_____

_____

_____

What are you thinking about? _____

_____

_____

_____

_____

_____

Reflect

What were your wins last week? _____

_____

_____

_____

_____

_____

What are you still working on? _____

_____

_____

_____

_____

What do you need to let go of? _____

_____

_____

_____

_____

Goal-Set

What do you need to complete in the week ahead? _____

_____

_____

_____

_____

_____

What do you need to work on? _____

_____

_____

_____

_____

_____

What are you thinking about? _____

_____

_____

_____

_____

Date:

Reflect

What were your wins last week? _____

_____

_____

_____

_____

_____

What are you still working on? _____

_____

_____

_____

_____

_____

What do you need to let go of? _____

_____

_____

_____

_____

_____

Goal-Set

What do you need to complete in the week ahead? _____

_____

_____

_____

_____

_____

What do you need to work on? _____

_____

_____

_____

_____

_____

What are you thinking about? _____

_____

_____

_____

_____

You can't do everything, but you can do something

Date:

Reflect

What were your wins last week? _____
_____
_____
_____
_____
_____

What are you still working on? _____
_____
_____
_____
_____
_____

What do you need to let go of? _____
_____
_____
_____
_____
_____

Goal-Set

What do you need to complete in the week ahead? _____

_____

_____

_____

_____

_____

What do you need to work on? _____

_____

_____

_____

_____

What are you thinking about? _____

_____

_____

_____

_____

Reflect

What were your wins last week? _____

_____

_____

_____

_____

_____

What are you still working on? _____

_____

_____

_____

_____

What do you need to let go of? _____

_____

_____

_____

_____

_____

Goal-Set

What do you need to complete in the week ahead? _____

_____
_____
_____
_____
_____

What do you need to work on? _____

_____
_____
_____
_____
_____

What are you thinking about? _____

_____
_____
_____
_____
_____

Date:

Reflect

What were your wins last week? _____

_____

_____

_____

_____

_____

What are you still working on? _____

_____

_____

_____

_____

_____

What do you need to let go of? _____

_____

_____

_____

_____

_____

Goal-Set

What do you need to complete in the week ahead? _____

_____

_____

_____

_____

_____

What do you need to work on? _____

_____

_____

_____

_____

_____

What are you thinking about? _____

_____

_____

_____

_____

Reflect

What were your wins last week? _____

_____

_____

_____

_____

_____

_____

What are you still working on? _____

_____

_____

_____

_____

_____

_____

What do you need to let go of? _____

_____

_____

_____

_____

_____

_____

Goal-Set

What do you need to complete in the week ahead? _____

_____

_____

_____

_____

_____

What do you need to work on? _____

_____

_____

_____

_____

What are you thinking about? _____

_____

_____

_____

_____

_____

You've got this

Reflect

What were your wins last week? _____

_____

_____

_____

_____

_____

What are you still working on? _____

_____

_____

_____

_____

What do you need to let go of? _____

_____

_____

_____

_____

Goal-Set

What do you need to complete in the week ahead? _____

_____

_____

_____

_____

_____

What do you need to work on? _____

_____

_____

_____

_____

What are you thinking about? _____

_____

_____

_____

_____

Date:

Reflect

What were your wins last week? _____

_____

_____

_____

_____

_____

What are you still working on? _____

_____

_____

_____

_____

_____

What do you need to let go of? _____

_____

_____

_____

_____

_____

Goal-Set

What do you need to complete in the week ahead? _____

_____

_____

_____

_____

_____

What do you need to work on? _____

_____

_____

_____

_____

_____

What are you thinking about? _____

_____

_____

_____

_____

_____

Date:

Reflect

What were your wins last week? _____

_____

_____

_____

_____

_____

What are you still working on? _____

_____

_____

_____

_____

What do you need to let go of? _____

_____

_____

_____

_____

Goal-Set

What do you need to complete in the week ahead? _____

_____

_____

_____

_____

_____

What do you need to work on? _____

_____

_____

_____

_____

_____

What are you thinking about? _____

_____

_____

_____

_____

_____

Date:

Reflect

What were your wins last week? _____

_____

_____

_____

_____

_____

What are you still working on? _____

_____

_____

_____

_____

What do you need to let go of? _____

_____

_____

_____

_____

Goal-Set

What do you need to complete in the week ahead? _____

_____

_____

_____

_____

_____

What do you need to work on? _____

_____

_____

_____

_____

_____

What are you thinking about? _____

_____

_____

_____

_____

_____

There is no right time

Date:

Reflect

What were your wins last week? _____
_____
_____
_____
_____
_____

What are you still working on? _____
_____
_____
_____
_____
_____

What do you need to let go of? _____
_____
_____
_____
_____
_____

Goal-Set

What do you need to complete in the week ahead? _____

_____

_____

_____

_____

_____

What do you need to work on? _____

_____

_____

_____

_____

_____

What are you thinking about? _____

_____

_____

_____

_____

_____

Reflect

What were your wins last week? _____
_____
_____
_____
_____
_____

What are you still working on? _____
_____
_____
_____
_____

What do you need to let go of? _____
_____
_____
_____
_____
_____

Goal-Set

What do you need to complete in the week ahead? _____

_____

_____

_____

_____

_____

What do you need to work on? _____

_____

_____

_____

_____

What are you thinking about? _____

_____

_____

_____

_____

Date:

Reflect

What were your wins last week? _____

_____

_____

_____

_____

_____

What are you still working on? _____

_____

_____

_____

_____

_____

What do you need to let go of? _____

_____

_____

_____

_____

_____

Goal-Set

What do you need to complete in the week ahead? _____

_____

_____

_____

_____

_____

What do you need to work on? _____

_____

_____

_____

_____

What are you thinking about? _____

_____

_____

_____

_____

Just start

Date:

Reflect

What were your wins last week? _____

_____

_____

_____

_____

_____

What are you still working on? _____

_____

_____

_____

_____

_____

What do you need to let go of? _____

_____

_____

_____

_____

Goal-Set

What do you need to complete in the week ahead? _____

_____

_____

_____

_____

_____

What do you need to work on? _____

_____

_____

_____

_____

_____

What are you thinking about? _____

_____

_____

_____

_____

_____

Date:

Reflect

What were your wins last week? _____

_____

_____

_____

_____

_____

_____

What are you still working on? _____

_____

_____

_____

_____

_____

_____

What do you need to let go of? _____

_____

_____

_____

_____

_____

_____

Goal-Set

What do you need to complete in the week ahead? _____

_____

_____

_____

_____

_____

What do you need to work on? _____

_____

_____

_____

_____

_____

What are you thinking about? _____

_____

_____

_____

_____

Date:

Reflect

What were your wins last week? _____

_____

_____

_____

_____

_____

What are you still working on? _____

_____

_____

_____

_____

_____

What do you need to let go of? _____

_____

_____

_____

_____

_____

Goal-Set

What do you need to complete in the week ahead? _____

_____

_____

_____

_____

_____

What do you need to work on? _____

_____

_____

_____

_____

_____

What are you thinking about? _____

_____

_____

_____

_____

Do the work

Reflect

What were your wins last week? _____

_____

_____

_____

_____

_____

What are you still working on? _____

_____

_____

_____

_____

What do you need to let go of? _____

_____

_____

_____

_____

_____

Goal-Set

What do you need to complete in the week ahead? _____

_____

_____

_____

_____

_____

What do you need to work on? _____

_____

_____

_____

_____

What are you thinking about? _____

_____

_____

_____

_____

Date:

Reflect

What were your wins last week? _____

_____
_____
_____
_____
_____

What are you still working on? _____

_____
_____
_____
_____
_____

What do you need to let go of? _____

_____
_____
_____
_____
_____

Goal-Set

What do you need to complete in the week ahead? _____

_____

_____

_____

_____

_____

What do you need to work on? _____

_____

_____

_____

_____

_____

What are you thinking about? _____

_____

_____

_____

_____

_____

Date:

Reflect

What were your wins last week? _____
_____
_____
_____
_____
_____

What are you still working on? _____
_____
_____
_____
_____
_____

What do you need to let go of? _____
_____
_____
_____
_____
_____

Goal-Set

What do you need to complete in the week ahead? _____

_____

_____

_____

_____

_____

What do you need to work on? _____

_____

_____

_____

_____

What are you thinking about? _____

_____

_____

_____

_____

It's never too late

Date:

Reflect

What were your wins last week? _____

_____
_____
_____
_____
_____

What are you still working on? _____

_____
_____
_____
_____
_____

What do you need to let go of? _____

_____
_____
_____
_____
_____

Goal-Set

What do you need to complete in the week ahead? _____

_____

_____

_____

_____

_____

What do you need to work on? _____

_____

_____

_____

_____

_____

What are you thinking about? _____

_____

_____

_____

_____

_____

Date:

Reflect

What were your wins last week? _____
_____
_____
_____
_____
_____

What are you still working on? _____
_____
_____
_____
_____
_____

What do you need to let go of? _____
_____
_____
_____
_____
_____

Goal-Set

What do you need to complete in the week ahead? _____

_____

_____

_____

_____

_____

What do you need to work on? _____

_____

_____

_____

_____

What are you thinking about? _____

_____

_____

_____

_____

Date:

Reflect

What were your wins last week? _____

_____

_____

_____

_____

_____

What are you still working on? _____

_____

_____

_____

_____

What do you need to let go of? _____

_____

_____

_____

_____

Goal-Set

What do you need to complete in the week ahead? _____

_____

_____

_____

_____

_____

What do you need to work on? _____

_____

_____

_____

_____

_____

What are you thinking about? _____

_____

_____

_____

_____

_____

Reflect

What were your wins last week? _____

_____

_____

_____

_____

_____

What are you still working on? _____

_____

_____

_____

_____

_____

What do you need to let go of? _____

_____

_____

_____

_____

_____

Goal-Set

What do you need to complete in the week ahead? _____

_____

_____

_____

_____

_____

What do you need to work on? _____

_____

_____

_____

_____

_____

What are you thinking about? _____

_____

_____

_____

_____

_____

Today is the day

Reflect

What were your wins last week? _____

_____

_____

_____

_____

_____

What are you still working on? _____

_____

_____

_____

_____

_____

What do you need to let go of? _____

_____

_____

_____

_____

_____

Goal-Set

What do you need to complete in the week ahead? _____

_____

_____

_____

_____

_____

What do you need to work on? _____

_____

_____

_____

_____

_____

What are you thinking about? _____

_____

_____

_____

_____

_____

Date:

Reflect

What were your wins last week? _____

_____

_____

_____

_____

_____

What are you still working on? _____

_____

_____

_____

_____

_____

What do you need to let go of? _____

_____

_____

_____

_____

_____

Goal-Set

What do you need to complete in the week ahead? _____

_____

_____

_____

_____

_____

What do you need to work on? _____

_____

_____

_____

_____

_____

What are you thinking about? _____

_____

_____

_____

_____

_____

Date:

Reflect

What were your wins last week? _____

_____

_____

_____

_____

_____

What are you still working on? _____

_____

_____

_____

_____

_____

What do you need to let go of? _____

_____

_____

_____

_____

_____

Goal-Set

What do you need to complete in the week ahead? _____

_____

_____

_____

_____

_____

What do you need to work on? _____

_____

_____

_____

_____

_____

What are you thinking about? _____

_____

_____

_____

_____

_____

Turn your ideas into actions

Date:

Reflect

What were your wins last week? _____
_____
_____
_____
_____
_____

What are you still working on? _____
_____
_____
_____
_____

What do you need to let go of? _____
_____
_____
_____
_____
_____

Goal-Set

What do you need to complete in the week ahead? _____

_____

_____

_____

_____

_____

What do you need to work on? _____

_____

_____

_____

_____

_____

What are you thinking about? _____

_____

_____

_____

_____

_____

Date:

Reflect

What were your wins last week? _____

_____

_____

_____

_____

_____

What are you still working on? _____

_____

_____

_____

_____

_____

What do you need to let go of? _____

_____

_____

_____

_____

_____

Goal-Set

What do you need to complete in the week ahead? _____

_____

_____

_____

_____

_____

What do you need to work on? _____

_____

_____

_____

_____

What are you thinking about? _____

_____

_____

_____

_____

Date:

Reflect

What were your wins last week? _____

_____

_____

_____

_____

_____

What are you still working on? _____

_____

_____

_____

_____

_____

What do you need to let go of? _____

_____

_____

_____

_____

Goal-Set

What do you need to complete in the week ahead? _____

_____

_____

_____

_____

_____

What do you need to work on? _____

_____

_____

_____

_____

_____

What are you thinking about? _____

_____

_____

_____

_____

_____

Big things happen one day at a time

Date:

Reflect

What were your wins last week? _____

_____

_____

_____

_____

_____

What are you still working on? _____

_____

_____

_____

_____

_____

What do you need to let go of? _____

_____

_____

_____

_____

_____

Goal-Set

What do you need to complete in the week ahead? _____

_____

_____

_____

_____

_____

What do you need to work on? _____

_____

_____

_____

_____

What are you thinking about? _____

_____

_____

_____

_____

Date:

Reflect

What were your wins last week? _____

_____

_____

_____

_____

_____

_____

What are you still working on? _____

_____

_____

_____

_____

_____

What do you need to let go of? _____

_____

_____

_____

_____

_____

Goal-Set

What do you need to complete in the week ahead? _____

_____

_____

_____

_____

_____

What do you need to work on? _____

_____

_____

_____

_____

_____

What are you thinking about? _____

_____

_____

_____

_____

_____

Date:

Reflect

What were your wins last week? _____

_____

_____

_____

_____

_____

What are you still working on? _____

_____

_____

_____

_____

_____

What do you need to let go of? _____

_____

_____

_____

_____

_____

Goal-Set

What do you need to complete in the week ahead? _____

_____
_____
_____
_____
_____

What do you need to work on? _____

_____
_____
_____
_____
_____

What are you thinking about? _____

_____
_____
_____
_____
_____

You can do this!

Reflect

What were your wins last week?

_____

_____

_____

_____

_____

_____

What are you still working on?

_____

_____

_____

_____

_____

_____

What do you need to let go of?

_____

_____

_____

_____

_____

_____

Goal-Set

What do you need to complete in the week ahead? _____

_____

_____

_____

_____

_____

What do you need to work on? _____

_____

_____

_____

_____

_____

What are you thinking about? _____

_____

_____

_____

_____

_____

Date:

Reflect

What were your wins last week? _____

_____

_____

_____

_____

_____

What are you still working on? _____

_____

_____

_____

_____

What do you need to let go of? _____

_____

_____

_____

_____

Goal-Set

What do you need to complete in the week ahead? _____

_____

_____

_____

_____

_____

What do you need to work on? _____

_____

_____

_____

_____

_____

What are you thinking about? _____

_____

_____

_____

_____

_____

Date:

Reflect

What were your wins last week? _____

_____

_____

_____

_____

_____

What are you still working on? _____

_____

_____

_____

_____

_____

What do you need to let go of? _____

_____

_____

_____

_____

_____

Goal-Set

What do you need to complete in the week ahead? _____

_____

_____

_____

_____

_____

What do you need to work on? _____

_____

_____

_____

_____

_____

What are you thinking about? _____

_____

_____

_____

_____

_____

Start at the beginning

Date:

Reflect

What were your wins last week? _____

_____

_____

_____

_____

_____

What are you still working on? _____

_____

_____

_____

_____

_____

What do you need to let go of? _____

_____

_____

_____

_____

_____

Goal-Set

What do you need to complete in the week ahead? _____

_____

_____

_____

_____

_____

What do you need to work on? _____

_____

_____

_____

_____

What are you thinking about? _____

_____

_____

_____

_____

Date:

Reflect

What were your wins last week? _____

_____

_____

_____

_____

_____

What are you still working on? _____

_____

_____

_____

_____

_____

What do you need to let go of? _____

_____

_____

_____

_____

_____

Goal-Set

What do you need to complete in the week ahead? _____

_____

_____

_____

_____

_____

What do you need to work on? _____

_____

_____

_____

_____

_____

What are you thinking about? _____

_____

_____

_____

_____

Date:

Reflect

What were your wins last week? _____

_____

_____

_____

_____

_____

What are you still working on? _____

_____

_____

_____

_____

What do you need to let go of? _____

_____

_____

_____

_____

_____

Goal-Set

What do you need to complete in the week ahead? _____

_____

_____

_____

_____

_____

What do you need to work on? _____

_____

_____

_____

_____

_____

What are you thinking about? _____

_____

_____

_____

_____

_____

Keep going